Anointed Thoughtz

I0200896

By:

TRINA HOLMES

ANOINTED THOUGHTZ

ANOINTED THOUGHTZ

Copyright © 2015 Trina Holmes

Printed in the United States of America

ISBN-13:978-0692548585
ISBN-10:0692548580

Printed by Createspace 2015
Published by BlaqRayn Publishing Plus 2015

Acknowledgments

First and foremost I want to think my heavenly father who made this all possible, I love you daddy and I can't see me doing anything without you in my life, thank you for giving me this gift of words, I owe this book all to you, thank you for the much needed Grace you have provided Me with.

I absolutely adore you, you gave me the courage and strength to believe in myself even when all odds was against me,I truly love you not only with words but with my life.

Secondly, I won't thank my lady bug my niece(Azarie) and my brother my heart beat (Freddie) Y'all believed in me when I didn't believe in myself and when no one would listen to my writing y'all listen, I love Y'all very much.

ANOINTED THOUGHTZ

*To my husband Tyhicus
Holmes thank you for the long
nights you stayed up with me
helping me prepare this book, I
just want to acknowledge my
family & Friends.*

*To my mother (Herticene
Sampson) and my father
(Frederick Douglas) thank y'all
for allowing God to use y'all to
give me life thank you both, My
sister's Falon Sampson,Tiffany
Sampson, Thank y'all so much
for the Love and support I love
y'all very much.*

*To my big sister and the oldest
(Ieshia Sampson) Wow I would
be forever writing about you, I
am extremely bless to have you
as a sister, when God created
you, he created a eagle and you
must understand the concept of
a eagle, Not only do a eagle fly
alone but a eagle fly very high
and can see though any kinda
weather, a eagle is very strong,
and a eagle is a protector,
sister you have protected and*

ANOINTED THOUGHTZ

*love me since I can remember,
you aided as mother in my life,
you taught me so much, and
you have accomplished so
much, There's not enough
words in the dictionary to
describe how much I appreciate
you, I love you very much
thank you so much for all you
have done and what you are
doing now.*

*To my brothers Antoine
Sampson, Darryl Sampson I
love you guys.*

*And to my Apostle Anna
Esther Poplous THANK you for
your Love and patient that you
have shown towards Me, thank
you for being my mother in the
gospel and teaching me the
truth, you have truly invested
your life in working for the
kingdom of God, You have
shown me what Christ look like
in the flesh, and for that I
appreciate God for creating
you.*

ANOINTED THOUGHTZ

To my Holy Remnant Family I love you all very much,To my very best friend Kiara Shackelford you have been there for me beyond what the world can fathom, it's so hard to come by authentic genuine people but God bless me with a covenant friend thank you and I love you.

And to my friend Shieka thank you for Listening to God that night when he gave you my poet name (Anointed Thoughtz) it was truly sent from above I love you very much, To my friend Susan thank you for showing me how Christ look like I love you, and to my friend Teresa thank you for always being there for me, I love you very much.

To my dearest friend James McCoy wow words can't express my gratitude towards you, You have deposited so much in me, but out of all the things you deposited, you

ANOINTED THOUGHTZ

taught me how to walk in excellent, and love the woman of God that I am, to love the skin I'm in, thank you very much and I love you.

To my sister from another mother Sandreesia you listen to me when I needed a shoulder to cry on, You never judge me, I love you for believing in me thank you.

To my niece and nephews Tete love Y'all If I have missed out anyone or any names thank you all from the bottom of my heart and may God bless you all.

Tablet of Content

ANOINTED THOUGHTZ

3. You are a Star
4. Man's World
5. Role Model
6. Dark Skin
7. Black Lies

My Love For Poetry

1. I love you poetry l
2. I love you poetry ll

Anointed Thoughtz

By:

TRINA HOLMES

ANOINTED THOUGHTZ

LOVE

I'm Not Perfect

I'm not perfect but I can love you perfectly, I hope you can see what God sees in me, I'm simplistic, the little things makes me smile, just a text to say how was your day, or a card, just saying you love me anyway , however, you got about your day, long as I'm on your mind, that's just fine with me, I hope you can see what God sees in me, because it would be ah shame if you would allow something as my imperfection get your way, of loving the best thing God made, remember I'm your rib, I'm apart of you, the heart of you, the essence of who you are as a man, can you look pass

my imperfection and love
me from deep within, I'm
not perfect but I can love
you perfectly.

Love On My Mind

I've got love on my mind
and there's nothing
particularly wrong, it's a
feelin I feel inside, when I
woke up early this
morning,it was staring me
straight in my eyes,

But I don't know if it's real
and I can't deal with the
fact that you lack in loving
me, see I know God love
me, but I don't question
that,   I question the fact
if I love myself, because
this love is whack, matters
of fact it's not you, its me,
I'm blind and can't see,
that I'm a diamond waiting
to be free, whatever you
put out there I take it, so I

deserve what you do to
me,but I also deserve to be
free, so I'm taking back
what the devil stole from
me, my dignity, my
integrity, my ability to see
that

I've got love on my mind,

and there's nothing
particularly wrong, it's a
feelin I feel inside, when I
woke up early this mornin,
it was starin me straight in
my eyes.

Me

Explore my mind and not
my body, the intimate
instruments of my heart,

Go into the deep parts,
where the blood flows,
from one blood vessel to
another, listen...to the
steel beats of life, do you
hear that, that's the sound
of life,

Go into my chromosome
which is my genetic,
magnetic, DNA, hey, it's
more to me than you think,
I'm not just a pretty face,
but you would be pretty
amaze, at my mind that's
connected to my soul, and
my soul is connected to
my Spirit and you got me.

I Used To Love Him

Cultivated by your touch
stimulated as much I used
To love him, but not as
much As he loved me, all
consuming was his love, it
felt like heaven from
above, I used to love
him,but Not as much as he
loved me,His love was
immaculate Perfectly
discreet, no one could ever
tell his love was so deep,I
used to love him but not
as much as he love me, out
of a million people I could
Distinguish him out of the
crowd,he stood proud and
Tall with full
confidence,That he would
conquer it all, I used to

love him,but not as much
As he loved me, he said

"Would you Do me the
honor of being my wife.. to
spend the rest of your life
with me and we be a
family.."

I used to love him, but not
as much as he loved me
because I didn't love me..

You love the real Me

I place my heart in your hands, and stand at command, and salute you, you didn't discard of my heart, like the rest did, but you played a major part, in giving me wisdom, and knowledge, I respect you as a man, a friend, that's why I take ah stand, and tell the whole world, you are the best, and I can't rest, without laying on your chest, love is so profound to you, I need to be around you At all times, there's not enough time in ah day for how I feel, love is in the way, eye to eye contact, transparency, you see me for just who I am, I

never had to be someone
else with you,I never had
to love less with you, I just
had to be exactly what I
was created to be, and
that's me.

Love Letter

I love him because he
understands that I'm a
woman, he caters to my
spirituality, I am a reality
in his world, he nos who
loves him so he don't have
to look no where else, Plus,
there's no one else, that
can compare to me, it's
only one me and he
sees,Who I can be and
push me to be greater
than he but he will always
be the head,because he
made his bed in my heart,
nothing can tear us apart,
so I play my part, and
allow him to be the man
and lead by GOD hand,one
day he will make me his
wife, and when that day
come, I will praise the

father, and tell him thank you for your son,your sent one, so I end this love letter, Remember we was place together in heaven, and now we are manifest in the flesh, so I rest, at the fact that you are God best.

Azarie

You believe in me when I couldn't see Azarie, you loved me, encourage me to believe in me, I owe you not my life, but my love Times 3, remember when you said Tete you can be anything you won't to be, just put your mind to it and you can do it, I looked at you like I knew it, that you will grow up and be Just like me, my blood flows though your body, so ladybugs thank you for loving me, you are my inspiration to keep writing freely, thank you for all the times you spit my piece, you almost spit better then me, that let me

I inspire you I love you so much I admire you, you

are my Angel sent from
God, I love you ladybug
you the real star.

I don't know You

I don't know you, I seen your face, and you smile is familiar, but your heart is not appealing, I made a big mistake in giving you my love, because you don't no what to do with a love that's from above, you been hurt so bad until the scars shows up where your smile use to be, and now all you think about is who you use to be, but now you just a use to be, and I use to be in love with you, but I realized it was never love, it was the thought of what I was use to, I'm sorry I don't know you, I seen your face before, but your heart never grow.

SPIRITUALITY

He Is

He makes me feel like a
lady, he internalize my
inner beauty, that no one
has ever paid attention to,
he looks past my flaws,
and cultivate my all, he's
is, the great I am, He
knows How to wipe away
my tears, that another
man put in my heart, he
loves all parts of me, even
the difficult parts, he
heals me, her reveals me,
he's strong, and outgoing,
courageous, amazin, he's
blazin, very contagious,
I'm affected by his
demeanor, his presence is
like no other, he's not like
any man, he's not hu~man,
he. is. God.

Without You

You are my oxygen, I can't see you but I know you there, is it fair to say, I can't breathe without you, I can't be without you, I can't see without you, me without you is like a ship without a sail,I don't want to live without you, because you are the reason for the season in my life, life without you is like a brain without the cells, bones without the skin, yes I'll let you in, because God I don't want to live my life without you, I love you..

Victory

Line upon Line, precept upon precept Life Is In The Hands Of The King Ring the bell of victory, in your life there's no mystery, what God can do, open your eyes and look at the world around you, can you see the king is do, killing, abortion, molestation, homosexuality, lesbianism, killing, abortion, molestation, homosexuality,lesbianism, digest the truth, and regurgitate it back up, line upon line, precept upon precept, can You except the king is on his way, any day now, let me say it again, molestation, rape,mental illness,

cancer, diabetes, murder,homosexuality,le sbianism, religion, broken marriages, infidelity, rejection, no compassion, lack of love, Hatred towards God, and he is are heart, but are heart is so hard, because the cares of the World harden are heart, GOD played his part in are life he made that ultimate sacrifice, but watch for the signs because he right on time.

Peculiar

You not like other girls, I
said because I live in a
peculiar world ah world
where girls like myself be
developed into
supernatural being, I
mean I love who he's
creating me to be, see, I no
the logic of multiplication
and elevation in the spirit,
yea here it, I know who I
am, just like you know
1+1=2 right, I know God
created me in his imagine
and like right, to live a
fulfilled life right, earth
get so boring i have to take
a trip to heaven, the
number 7 is the number of
completions, I'm deleting
the negativity out my life
right, the devil thought he
had my life.. sike, I did a

upper cut on the devil in the spirit like Mike, Tyson is a brand of food, but I'm a brand all by myself I thought you new, trueeeeeeeee, so to answer your question no I'm not like other girls, I was born into this world but I'm a special type of girl hand made by the king himself, yessss, I love who I am because before I was a hot mess.

Rejection

Bullet wounds to her heart
the pain has in large her
heart, tears has flooded
her face like a tsunami
because of the bombing of
life, insecurity was her
security blanket, and as
she tried to sleep away the
pain, rain continually to
fall down on her, pain
continues to follow her
and games continues to
play her, her body was a
lethal weapon and she use
it to kill, steal, and destroy,
and God nos her body
made a lot of noise, like
somebody just love Me,
and like somebody notice
me please, love just love
me, she was internally
bleeding and internally
needing someone to fill

that void in her life, premeditated thoughts of suicide but she still rises, this is a life of a wounded soul, so please let's continue to pray for the lost, because her can be you at any cost.

Open Wounds

Wounds in the way un
purified sores heart filled
with so much hurt from
the time you came into
this world, doubtful
disgraceful, unfaithful
disloyal people has
tampered with your
psyche because they
psyche has no stability
credibility,sincerely,they
are life takers they try to
take your breathe away,
but inhale exhale...
Breathe God sees and
here's your cry say
goodbye to the grand
Reaper, because you shall
live and not die,and
prepare to fly, like the
Eagle up up up and away
better days is ahead of you,
God is ahead you,they

mad at you BECAUSE YOU
ARE SUCCESSFUL, so rest
assure your day are full
because of the one and
only creator The most
high.

The Joy of the Lord

My heart beats for you,
there's a seat in my Spirit
that leaps for you, the joy
of Lord is my straight,
happy days are here again,
because I'm in the vain Of
the king, wash me in your
blood clean me up, and
give me all your Love, I'm
yours, I belong to you, I
long for you, I write this
song for You, and sing the
joy of the Lord is my
straight, the joy of the
Lord is my straight , oh
how wonderful is the Love
of the king, who were the
royal ring, his clothes is
made of Righteousness,
his smile is made of love,
and his spirit fits me like a
glove, send down the
doves, and listen to the

Lily sing a sweet song, a
song of gladness, a new
song,
I will continue to sing the
joy of the Lord is my
straight, the joy of the
Lord is my straight, make
way for the sovereign
King,roll out the red
carpet, pave the way the
king is on his way, call for
the the horse and chariot,
can you see the king today,
I Will sing the joy of the
Lord is my straight.

One New Man

Can we come together the
Jews and the gentile for
one common purpose, to
celebrate are Christ in the
land that's flowing with
milk and honey, and be
Excited and exuberant
that are master lives
forever We are call one
new man this will last
forever, understand,are
culture its not black or
white, blue or green, We
are the culture of the king,
in his eyes there is know
color all he see is Citizens
of the kingdom, if the
Jews walks in obedience,
and the gentiles do to
What makes us different,
both walks must be True,
Not true in words but true
in deeds..

We can't walk for God
and can't fall on are knees,
And humble are self in the
Present of the king, and
cry holy holy How holy
you are thank You for
in-grafting us, we shooting
for the star, now the only
thing separate us from
each other is are mind set,
set your mind to believe
the truth because the
truth shell set you free, we
have the same blood line
holy, no longer are We two
this is true, we're one new
man I thought you knew.

CONSCIOUS

Dysfunctional Man

He aggressively place his
hands on me, and told me
he love me,characterize by
his lies,demise his touch,
o how I want to hate him
so much, but as much as I
want to, I can't because
women we must
understand a
dysfunctional man.
Life for him was
unpredictable, but so
predictable, he live a
complicated miss
educated life that's right,
yes he is a man that has
became a product of his
environment,
alignment,assignment of
life,only to make it
right,he never ask to be

born into this life,but since he's here,he fears to be alone please don't leave me alone, baby come back home,I'm sorry for the way that I treated you but please understand I been abuse, abuse by the system and program by the world It's impossible for him to love his girl, But he conveys a message to the world that I'm strong, and it's alright to hit my girl, because of the function in my world, but its not..

It's a function of a dysfunction man that never had the chance to be rise by a real man,day in night, night and day, he cries,because of the lies that was told to him,sold to him, unfold to him, how do he deal with the pain of the rain in his life, he can't make her his wife, until he see,he was born into a dysfunctional family, and except the fact he need to grow, and let all the pain go, that has been hunted him for so long its time to move on stand up for your rights, and fight, for your life,because you are the epitome of God eyes, there is nothing more beautiful then a man, that understand, that he was created to love his woman.

A Mother

The rage of a woman
that's been hurt by her
mother, anger, frustration,
manipulation, agitation,
regurgitate, those words
up that she spoke over her
life, like she will never be
nothing, or like she won't
go far in life, she resent
those words,not in
consent with those words,
but she wants her mother
to be proud of her
accomplishments,
achievements, even in her
time of bereavement, the
state of loss in her life, she
wants her mother to
sacrifice, and just
CONGRATULATE her for
once or twice that would
be nice, but she Don't
understand why her

mother want acknowledge
her as being a woman,
that's because her mother
mother never taught her
to be a woman, a woman
begotten a woman, A
mother is good as what
she know, so she doesn't
blame her mother
anymore, she takes it
strive and grow, because
she was never taught to be
a mother.

You are a Star

Why do you hate the skin
you in, is it because you
never was taught to love
from within, without a
shadow of a doubt, you
don't no who you are,
cause if you did you would
Reprogram your mind into
believing the true star you
are, but because you been
brain washed you can't
wash away the seed they
planted in your psyche,
now you walking around
like Mikey, eating up all
the lies they told you, sold
you slavery, but who the
son set free is free indeed,
lately I been feeling like I
want to Expose the truth
For what it Really is, but
can you handle the truth
For who really are, you are

more then what man told
you, you are a star..

Man's World

I could never understand a
man his hurts,his pain,
that's far from my lane,
his mood,his rude, it's
time to exclude myself out
the picture Lady's we been
missing, the point of the
matter, is that a man has a
weight to carry when
sometimes he can barely
hold his head up high,
why he ask? is life this
hard, I do my part in
society,but still I can't get
far, because the system
was meant to hold you
down keep you around in
darkness there's no light,
it's hard to fight when he
can't see at night, he
wishes he can take a fight,
to a far far place,where he
want be judged by his

face,and his skin, this pain is deep within so he hold his tears, and keep his fears all to himself,he can't love for him self so he tries to love someone else, but it's wrong, because there's an purified wounds, filled with poison venom all in him, so lady's please cry for our babies, yes he is baby because it took a woman to have a baby, and then he became a man child, and now that he is a man he still is your child, to conclude this matter, please let's pray for our man they made the world we live in, this a man's world but it wouldn't be nothing without a woman or a girl.

Role Model

I watch him as he awoke
Early in the morning,
Yawning wiping cold Out
his eye saying baby Get up
it time for school No
breaking the rules, you
Got to be the next,doctor,
Or lawyer but whatever,
You choose to be,make
sure you be the best at it,
Never quit at it, I just want
to push you to your full
potentials, I watched him
comb her hair, lay out her
clothes, make her
breakfast, only God
no's,The love ah father has
for His daughter it's like
no other, I paid close
attention to him, I thought
to myself I want my
Husband to be just like
him, He was my role

model, I watch him sit up in cry Because some day he didn't No how we was gonna get by And drop to his knees begging God please, help me and my baby Girl get though the day, he was my role models and I model his role.

Dark Skin

He said you was pretty to
be a dark skin girl but
dark skin Not accepted In
his would, only light
bright Is what I'm dealing
with tonight, Because of
the stories I heard About
dark skin people..

How could they be my
equal, I'm so much better
than that as a matter of
fact, they still got whips
on there back, I said it And
I won't take it back, its a
known fact that light is
better Than dark, call it
what you will, But my
mind has been Instilled to
believe that about all dark
skin people, how could
they be my equal, he said I
was pretty to be a dark

skin girl, but I said to him my skin is not validated by

The opinion of man, for you are only Human, not God my Friend,so how you Feel about me, doesn't matter to me, Because God created me, and who the son set free is free Indeed, so I'll take me and my dark skin, love myself from within,and while you hating yourself..

I pray that when you look in the mirror and see that you are the same color as me,begin to Love who God created you to be,

Remember you said I'm pretty to be a Dark skin girl but your skin is dark to, but in your mind your skin is light because you

have not accepted the fact
that you're black, you said
I was pretty to be a dark
skin girl Remember that.

Black Lies

Black, black, lies, about,
color, kings, let me
reiterate that to the men,
black, lies, about, color,
kings, as in the European
lied to are man, and told
them that they was good
for nothing, worthless,
untitled, untold, sold into
slavery, the more we slave
you, the more y'all
producing babies, and not
to mention the Willie
Lynch letter, that got our
pockets getting fatter, and
fatter, because of a mental
slavery letter, now y'all
killing each other, and we
sitting back laughing at
y'all, ha-ha we cashing
y'all out, tagging y'all out,
don't act surprise like y'all

didn't no y'all was up for sell, mental jail, cell block ,$1.00 for the big black man to the right he'll pick yo Cotton all night, going once going twice sold to the old white man who so kindly gave me $1.01for this negro, with the big afro, so let us define black according to the dictionary, the European dictionary that is, lets see,you got dirt and midnight, are they comparing you to a black shirt, you got gloom and doom, there's no room, in this world they say, for a black man that can die any day, because of the lack of knowledge of who they are, why go far, now hold up, hold up, hold up now, check this out, they define you as harmful and hostile,

OMG, but so surreal you see, because they program your mind into believing the lie, they told you about yourself, to doubt yourselves, so you want fly, like the eagle, and use your all seeing eye, black, black, lies, about, colored, kings, they don't want you to see who you was really meant to be, cause if you ever come to reality, you would be a threat to society, o no they can't allow that to be, o no they can't allow you to see, the royalty in thee, your roots are rich, and you breed from the genealogy of king David, but if they can keep you blindfolded so you can't see, it would be the blind leading the blind, now that's victory, in the eye's of the enemy, black,

black, lies, about, colored,
kings, but you will always
be the real king to me...

My Love For Poetry

Poetry I

Poetry: When did you fall in love with me.

Me: At the tender age of 3 but I didn't start writing you until I was able to understand, that writing is in high demand, I love everything about you,From your spoken word, nouns, and verbs, From your gentle touch, oh do I love you so much, especially the aggressive part of you, that's the heart of you, and how you

articulate, everyone is able to relate, I really love the Fact that it's a lot of truth in that, which you stand for, demand for, people to pay close attention to you, or miss ah essential part of you, sometimes you can be

Inconsiderate tho, but that's only for the people to grow, because sometimes they don't understand your vocabulary, however you go about deliberating your message it's a message From your heart,so you see my love For you is freely given, that's because I love poetry.

Poetry: I love you too

Poetry II

Positive motivation in my life, you only speak life, once or twice I might have head you speak not to nice, but other then that you my better half , other half, I'm only half the women without you, but with you I'm whole, we are one not two, or three, fold, one thing for certain, two things for sure, this is are year, I refuse to live without you, you are very soft spoken, ah token, of my love, I love you poetry...

About the Author

Trina Holmes was born and raised in Chicago. She enjoys writing poetry and short stories as well as singing and playing the keyboard and guitar. She was 17 years old when she discovered she had a love and gift for poetry and writing.

She began putting her thoughts on paper creating a collage of short stories and poems. It wasn't until December of 2013 that her writing and poetry would be before a broader audience.

Trina and a friend went to a poetry set for the first time and the experience opened a world of possibilities for her. It was the same fateful night that Trina was given her stage name "**Anointed Thoughtz**" and from there on a star was born.

The God-given name stuck and Anointed Thoughtz has graced and performed on over 50 stages in the Chicago area. She had been featured at various well- known poetry venues in Chicago such as **Hot Sauce Poetry, The Sanctuary, Word of War, Soul Fusion , Strictly for Listeners and Set it off** just to name a few.

She became a co-host for Chicago Fire online poetry radio show which led to her co-hosting her own show "Well Spoken" with long time friend, another notable Chicago poet **Eddie Fulton known as Word Warrior.**

ANOINTED THOUGHTZ

Due to her fame through out the poetry scene, Anointed Thoughtz was invited to perform on Chicago's very own 1570 am live radio in honor of **Maya Angelou. Anointed Thoughtz** is currently writing her first book of poetry which is self-titled "**Anointed Thoughtz**" which will be released in the fall of 2015.